IBIZA

Editorial Escudo de Oro, S.A.

The port.

IBIZA AND FORMENTERA

Introduction

Ibiza, the «White Isle», lies in the heart of the western Mediterranean. The cosmopolitan atmosphere which envelops its capital and coastlines contrasts with the rural traditions of the interior. Even today, one can still catch a glimpse of country life and of surviving traces of the hippy culture of the 1960s. Ibiza is visited nowadays by young people, by the «beautiful people» and by the «jet-set». The island is one continuous party, a multifarious spectacle of people from all four corners of the world and, at the same time, a refuge of craftsmen, painters and sculptors, who come here in search of the undescribable light found in the *Islas Pitiusas,* as these islands are known here.

Geography and climate

Ibiza is situated southwest of the coast of Spain, 100 nautical miles from Valencia. With an area of 572 km², it is the third largest of the Balearic Islands, after Majorca and Minorca. Along with Formentera and other smaller islets, it forms the Archipelago of Las Pitiusas, a name of Greek origin which refers to the many pine woods which covered these isles in remote times. Ibiza is well-communicated both by sea and by air. Regular flights connect it with Alicante, Barcelona, Madrid, Valencia and Palma de Mallorca, whilst various companies ply the sea routes between the island and Barcelona, Denia, Valencia and Majorca, carrying passengers and vehicles. Formentera, not having its own airport, is connected to the largest of the Pitiusas by many ferries and fast launches. The Pitiusas enjoy a dry, sunny climate with very little rainfall (less than 450 mm per year) and relative humidity of around 70%. Average annual temperature is around 18 degrees Centigrade.

La Penya and Dalt Vila.

Monument to
Vara de Rey

Plaza del
Parque.

Paseo Juan Carlos I.

Historic background

Innumerable peoples and groups have left their mark on the island, from the first settlers of prehistoric times to the hippies of the 1960s, combining to create a veritable melting-pot of cultures which is reflected in the cosmopolitan atmosphere of Ibiza and which is not found on any other of the islands of the Balearic archipelago. The name «Ibiza» comes from the Punic world «Ybshm», meaning «Island of Bes», the divinity venerated by the Carthaginians. The island's

privileged situation led to its being colonised in the mid-7th century BC by Phoenicians from the Straits of Gibraltar area. In the late-6th century BC, the island fell under the influence of Carthage and fresh groups of settlers joined the Phoenician communities already established here, with consequent occupation of the entire territory and notable growth of the only city on the islands, which then had a population of just a few thousand inhabitants. This population increase stimulated exploitation of the island's resources

Dalt Vila.

-wine, oil and salt - and led to the establishment of a large number of rural enterprises. At the same time, the city of Ibiza was gaining in importance within the Mediterranean region, becoming a centre for the distribution of the goods of Phoenicians, Etruscans, Greeks and Egyptians to the Iberian Peninsula. The intense commercial activity of Ibiza is shown clearly not only by the abundance of pottery containers (amphoras) from the island found throughout the western Mediterranean, but also by the wide distribution of Ebusitan coins. The island's coins were not only used in trade, but also formed part of funeral offerings, as well as being used for adornment and as protective amulets. From the second half of the 4th century BC onwards, a large trade infrastructure was established between Ibiza and the Phoenicians, with the creation of coastal trading stations such as that on the isle of Na Guardis off the coast of Majorca, from where intensive exchanges were established with the indigenous Talayot community, including the recruit-

Plaza Reina Sofía and Portal Nou

Plaza Dalt Vila.

The entrance to Dalt Vila.

The Castle of Dalt Vila.

Typical view of Dalt Vila.

Ibiza from the viewpoint of Plaza de la Catedral.

ment of mercenaries («Honderos») for the Carthaginian armies. After the Second Punic War, «Ybshm» enjoyed a period of plenitude and development. Foreign trade reached its maximum level, only to decline when the capital became federated with Rome, the island becoming known to the Romans as Ebusus. In around 25 BC, the last Punic phase began, Romanisation became accentuated and finally, in the year 74 AD, Ibiza lost its status as a federated city to become «Municipio Flavio Ebusitano», integrated into Tarra-gona province as part of the Roman Empire. Latin became the official language, gradually establishing itself as the local vernacular. After the Low Roman Empire (245-455 AD), the island was occupied firstly by Vandals (455-534) and then by the Byzantines (after 534). In the 10th century, the Balearic Islands were conquered by the Moorish forces under Al-Jawlani (902-3) and annexed to the Cordova caliphate. It later formed part of the Kingdom of Denia, before gaining independence (1059-1115). Finally, the archi-

A fine view of Dalt Vila.

pelago was annexed firstly to the Almoravide Empire and then conquered by the Almohades. The Moorish period ended with the conquest of the islands by Aragon in 1235. Later still, Ibiza and Formentera formed part of the Kingdom of Majorca (1276-1343) before being absorbed by the Kingdom of Catalonia-Aragon and, finally, Spain. The 16th and 17th centuries were marked by continuous attacks by Turkish and Barbary Coast pirates, by the onslaught of the plague, which caused huge mortality, and by

long periods of famine due to failed harvests. All this caused grave conflicts between the people of the country and the inhabitants of the city. In the 18th century, Ibiza lost all its privileges with the imposition of the Bourbon dynasty in the figure of King Philip V. The «Universitat» (organ of self-government) was dissolved and the salt mines became crown property. The year 1739 saw the commencement of the activities of the corsairs, action prolonged until 1828, when the crown ordered the disarming of all ships engaged in

Cathedral front.

privateering. In 1782, Ibiza received its city charter, enabling it to establish the bishopric. However, it was from the 1960s on that the island underwent the most important change in recent centuries, being transformed from poor lands, from which it was often necessary to emigrate, to a place of immigration due to the need to cover the demand for services generated by growing domestic and international tourism.

Interior of the cathedral.

A night-time view of Ibiza.

Restaurant in the La Marina district, the casino and a taste of the night-time atmosphere at the port.

The capital

The island's capital, **Ibiza,** or **Eivissa,** as it is known in Catalan, was founded by the Phoenicians in 654 BC. The urban layout of the city was determined in the 6th century BC: an acropolis surrounded by strong walls, the trading area around the harbour (now La Marina and Sa Penya), the necropolis in Puig des Molins, at the foot of which grew up the potters' quarter. It was here that pottery, terra cotta figures and moulds for producing plaques representing the god Bes and busts of the goddess Tanit were made. By the 5th century BC, Eivissa had developed into an important urban centre with a population of around 5,000 people. The city now has over 30,000 inhabitants, but its physiognomy continues to be spectacular. Dalt Vila, the highest part of the city, ancient and monumental, is reached through the gate known as El Portal de les Taules. This quarter conserves Renaissance-style walls dating to the 16th century and designed by the Italian architect Giovanni Battista Calvi. As we have said, El Portal de les Taules, a monumental gate overlooking the port, is the main entrance to the old city. It is crowned by a huge shield bearing the coat of arms of Philip II and flanked by reproductions of two Roman statues. The steep climb up from here leads us to the castle, the

The Botafoch lighthouse, with Ibiza in the background.

Gothic cathedral, whose origins go back to the 13th century, and the Archaeological Museum, which contains a veritable treasure of Punic art. The cathedral sacristy houses the Diocesan Museum, whose outstanding exhibit is a gilt silver monstrance featuring a reproduction of a 14th-century Gothic tower, the Altarpiece of Sant Gregori, made up of a series of panels painted in the 15th and 16th centuries, and other liturgical objects. Before returning beyond the walls, we can visit the Museum of Contemporary Art, installed in a former arsenal and magazine, constructed in 1727 ac-cording to the design drawn up by the engineer Simon Poulet) or the church of the former Convent of Santo Domingo (17th century) with its fine Altarpiece of Nostra Senyora del Rosari and a number of other interesting paintings, mostly baroque in style. This is the only church on these islands which has a cloister. The exterior view of this site is fascinating, the tiles of the domes of various chapels configuring one of Dalt Vila's most characteristic silhouettes. Splendid views can be enjoyed from any of the baluarts (those of Santa Llúcia, Santa Tecla, Sant Bernat, Sant Jordi, Santiago,

Sant Pere or Sant Joan), or from the lovely viewpoint of the City Hall, a splendid balcony overlooking the Mediterranean. The terraces of the bars in Plaìa de la Vila invite one to stop for a refreshing drink, whilst the many shops and art galleries here are a constant temptation to buy. This zone also contains El Corsario, a 17th-century house formerly inhabited by the famous corsair, Antonio Riquer, now a charming hotel. Leaving the old quarter through the Portal Nou, we come to the modern part of the city. It is pleasant to stroll around La Marina, formerly occupied by fishermen and tradesmen and the site of the obelisk commemorating the heroic Ibizan corsairs who confronted the Moorish pirates in many battles, and the elegant Passeig de Vara de Rey (named after a hero of the Cuban War), or to discover unusual nooks and crannies in the narrow streets and tiny squares of the seaboard Sa Penya quarter. Those wishing to learn more about the Punic period will be impressed by a visit to the Puig des Molins Museum, just off

The cruiser Oriana.

Two views of Talamanca.

Aerial view of Cala Llonga.

Avinguda d'Espanya. The name Puig des Molins («hill of mills») is a reference to the many windmills which formerly stood on the top of this promontory, whose central area was used as the city necropolis from the Phoenician period until the time of the Roman Empire. In the 5th century BC, an area of the necropolis measuring over 50,000 m^2 was used for burials in hypogea (underground chambers carved into the rock). This is one of the most important archaeological sites on the Pitiusas, declared a monument of historic and artistic interest in 1931.

The coasts and hills of Ibiza

Although in summer the central streets of the capital are a veritable «human circus» and certain areas of the coast have become tourist ghettoes in which blocks of cement and souvenir shops predominate, the entire interior of the island, with its half dozen white villages, continues to live in tune with its traditional rhythm. We shall begin our tour by leaving Eivissa in a northeasterly direction, curving round the harbour to reach the nearest beach, **Talamanca,** a

Cala Llonga beach.

Overall view of «La Siesta».

Santa Eulalia del Río: Riomar.

broad expanse of sand with small hotels, sailing and windsurfing schools and many other opportunities for nautical activities. Continuing towards Santa Eulàlia, the road turns inland, passing through the tiny village of **Jesús,** in whose cemetery is buried the Catalan architect Josep Lluís Sert, powerfully enamoured of the island and the designer of the headquarters of the local architects' college, constructed in 1964 in the upper zone of the capital. The Gothic Church of Jesús, whose origins go back to 1466, was occupied first by Franciscan and then by Dominican monks, the latter later moving to Dalt Vila, where they built the Convent of Santo Domingo. The church has a plain, unadorned façade, with a side porch at the eastern end. The interior has a nave with three chapels on either side. In the presbytery, covered by a Gothic vault and features a good 15th-century altarpiece from the Valencian workshop of Rodrigo de Osona. From Jesús, the road runs through gentle hills and pinewoods, passing close to the **Roca Llisa** residential area, a haven for golf

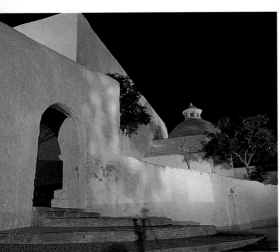

*Santa Eulalia del Río: Plaza de
España, Puig de Missa and the
fountain in the Paseo Marítimo.*

Santa Eulalia del Río beach.

lovers. We then descend towards the **Cala Llonga** development, an important tourist centre, to **Saint Eulària d'es Riu,** which lies on a fertile plain dotted with vegetable gardens. The name of Ibiza's second largest city, with 17,000 inhabitants, refers to its first chapel, founded in the 13th century and devoted to the saint of the same name, and the only river on the island. Until the arrival of the first tourists in the 1960s, the local economy was chiefly based on agriculture. Despite the urban transformation of the coastline caused by the massive construction of tourist accommodation, Saint Eulària still conserves the air of a restful city, in which a gentle stroll and a chat form an essential part of daily life. The most characteristic feature of the locality is the Puig de Missa, a tiny hill reaching to 52 metres above sea level, crowned by a 16th-century fortified church. This has a magnificent arcade with three rows of semicircular arches, a semicircular bastion attributed to Giovanni Battista Calvi and two

Cala Pada.

dark-coloured domes. Around the church huddle the houses of the original town centre whilst opposite is the Barrau Museum, a tiny monographic museum dedicated to the Catalan painter Laureà Barrau (1863-1957). Another interesting collection was opened to the public in 1994, after the Can Ros farmhouse had been restored by the Island Council and the «Islas Baleares» Foundation. This is the Ethnological Museum of the Pitiusa Islands, whose exhibits make up a representative display of the tradi-

tional culture of the island, from valuable jewels forming part of the «emprendades» to a vast variety of objects used in different trades and folkloric elements. After such edifying visits, a pleasant stroll is needed, passing through Plaça de l'Ajuntament to La Rambla and down to the sea to enjoy a meal at one of the many typical restaurants. Saint Eulària d'es Riu has an excellent pleasure port and a popular beach adjoining the city centre itself. Just a few kilometres away, along the coast road, are

*Punta Arabí Club and two views of the
Es Canar market.*

Two views of Es Canar.

Overall view of Es Canar.

such havens of calm as peaceful **Cala Pada,** as well as busy **Es Canar,** a large tourist resort where every Wednesday the **Punta Arabí** market, the most important weekly market on the island, takes place. The environs of Es Canar include **Cala Nova, Cala Llenya** and the picturesque beach of **Niu Blau.** Having visited this coastal attraction, we must now return inland to **Sant Carles de Peralta,** whose main square boasts an 18th-century church with elegant portico crowned by a modest belltower.

An important meeting-point for locals, holiday-makers and artists alike is the Bar Anita, behind this church. The Las Dalias market, held here every Saturday, conserves all the flavour of the times of the hippy generation. Many roads lead back to the coast from here so that we can bathe in one or other of the most charming coves of the entire coastline of Ibiza: tiny **Cala Boix** and peaceful **Cala Mastella** to the south and the broad beaches of **Es Figueral** and **Aigües Blanques** to the north.

Aerial view of Cala Nova.

Partial view of Cala Llenya.

Niu Blau.

Further north still is **Cap Roig,** where the tower known as Torre de'n Valls, popularly known as Torre de Campanitx, stands, one of the ten coastal defense towers surviving from the 18th century, restored in 1982. The tower has a doorless ground floor, a vaulted main floor and upper defense platform. From Cap Roig it is possible to make out the tall silhouette of **Tagomago,** a privately-owned islet offering yachts and other small boats beautiful anchorages of white sand. The little-used road from Sant Carles to **Cala de Sant Vicent** offers splendid views of the sea through its pinewoods. Sant Vicent, nowadays a popular tourist resort, has an extensive beach protected from the north winds by **Punta Grossa.** In nearby **Cova d'es Cuilleram** (now closed to the public), where the goddess Tanit was worshipped, archaeological excavations in 1907 unearthed a huge quantity of objects dating back to the Punic period, amongst them a terra-cotta bust representing Tanit adorned with a winged

The church at Sant Carles de Peralta.

mantle, a *kalathos* on her head. This piece is displayed at the Archaeological Museum in Eivissa. The tiny Church of Sant Vicent de Sa Cala, completed in the first half of the 19th century, is the most modern on the island. The road now leaves the northernmost littoral to take us inland to a fertile valley and **Sant Joan,** a village nestling between mountains and containing the Church of Sant Joan de Labritja, completed in 1732. The C-733 road now takes us back to the northern coast. **Portinatx,** with its beaches at **S'Arenal Gran** and **S'Arenal Petit,** is an authentically natural harbour, used as such centuries ago by Phoenician traders. Beside it is **Cala Xaraca,** a cove of crystalline waters, and the Torre de Portinatx, a coastal defense tower, its circular body crowned by a cone-shaped section. It was designed by the engineer Ballester and built by García Martínez in 1763. Returning to the village of Sant Joan, following the same road inland, we come to **Sant Llorenç de Balàfia,** a locality of great ar-

Cala Boix.

*Es Figueral
beach.*

Aeries view of Es Figueral.

tistic interest thanks to its church and the rural architectural site of Balàfia. The church was the second in the «cuartón» of Santa Eulària. The decision to build it was taken in the first half of the 18th century, and it was inaugurated in 1797. The interior is reached through a rectangular porch and consists of a single nave covered by a barrel vault. Nearby is a country track leading to Can Pere Mosson, whose high tower of red-

Aigües Blanques beach.

Overall view of Cala San Vicente.

dish stone contrasts with the shining brightness of the whitewashed walls. A short distance away is the fortified rural hamlet of Balàfia, a unique site consisting of five houses separated by neat flower and vegetable gardens and flanked by two protecting towers. In Balàfia are conserved fountains, ovens and many other architectural elements going back thousands of years. Returning to the country road, we now come to **Santa Gertrudis de Fruitera,** one of the most peaceful villages in Ibiza, with its tiny craft and antique shops,

bars and restaurants which attract the local chic society. Northwards once more, we reach **Sant Miquel de Balansat,** a village dominated by a white-walled 14th-century fortified church. At the top of a steep rise we enter the broad patio where traditional dancing takes place every week. From here, we enter a spacious portico opening up in front of the main door. The nave is supported by Gothic arches dating back to the original construction. The most interesting feature is, perhaps, the side chapel of Benirràs where some years ago

Portinatx beach.

were discovered, under the paint-work, frescoes dating back to the year 1690, giving rise to its popular name of the «chapel of the paintings». On the opposite side is the Chapel of El Roser, built by Bishop Mora in order to give the groundplan of the church the shape of a cross. Four kilometres separate the original village of San Miquel from its port, **Port de San Miquel,** a bay surrounded by cliffs now disfigured by massive buildings. Nearby, in a pleasant residential zone, is one of the island's architectural jewels: the Hotel Hacienda Na Xamena. This, Ibiza's only five-star hotel, is in the purest Ibizan style, standing at the top of a high promontory surrounded by luxuriant pinewoods. In the environs of Port de San Miquel is La Cova de Can Marça, reached along a path carved into the rock which leads to the cave entrance via a viewpoint commanding views of the entire bay, with the **Isle of Murada** in the background. This islet is the habitat of the muradensis lizard, an endemic species

Two views of Portinatx.

Cala Xarraca.

of bright colours. The cave is over 100,000 years in age, and inside it the bones and fossils of extinct species have been found. It was used in the pas by smugglers to hide their illegal wares. Another highly-recommended· excursion is to **Cala Benirràs,** a peaceful beach in one of the best areas for underwater swimming on the entire northern coastline, reached by an unmetalled road. Here, divers will find an extraordinary wealth of things to see, including the remains of a shipwreck at a depth of 38 metres at the entrance to the cove.

In the northwest zone of the island, an almost completely virgin area known as **Els Amunts,** are solitary landscapes, small villages unchanged over the years and a richness of rural architecture, with brightly-whitewashed cube-shaped houses. Narrow roads join Sant Miquel de Balansat with the isolated country churches of **Sant Mateu d'Albarca** and **Santa Agnès de Corona,** far from the great centres of population and the more conventional tourist resorts. The origins of the Church of Sant Mateu d'Albarca go back to a

Port de Sant Miguel.

decree issued in 1785 by the first bishop of Las Pitiusas, Manuel Abad y Lasierra, establishing the parish of Sant Mateu. The church was finished in 1796, whilst the bullrush - by the maestros Cova and Cires - dates back to the year 1861, and the porch was added during the 1890s. Off the nave are the chapels of the Virgen de Montserrat and of El Rosario, on the right of the presbytery, whilst opposite are those of El Corazón

Sant Miquel de Balansant: church.

Cala Salada.

Cala Grassió.

Sea front, Sant Antoni.

de Jesús, San Vicente, La Virgen del Carmen, San Juan y San Jaime. This route around the most traditional area of the island terminates at the bustling little city of **Sant Antoni de Portmany.** The old Portus Magnus of the Romans is nowadays the third-largest centre of population (15,000 inhabitants) and the largest tourist resort on the island, attracting mostly young, predominantly British visitors. In the harbour, numerous boats offer tourists trips to the beaches of the west coast, whilst the sea front is lined with open-air cafés and the more recent addition of the curious sculpture of «Columbus' Egg», an avant-garde creation. The historic centre features one of the five oldest churches on the island, dating back to the 14th century. In 1305, the inhabitants of Sant Antoni de Portmany requested permission from the archbishop of Tarragona to build a chapel and a cemetery, possibly on the same site as that now occupied by this church. The original construction, of which the presbytery remains, was greatly modified in the 17th century, when the tower, main door

*Partial view
of La Vila de
Sant Antoni.*

*Sant Antoni:
church.*

Two views of the Bay of Sant Antoni.

and choir were built. In the early-18th century, the rectory over the church was completed, though this was converted into a side patio in the 19th century. The church contains various fine art works, including the painting of «The Ecstasy of Saint Anthony», the 18th-century statue of the «Virgin of the Rosary» and the 17th-century carving of Saint Vincent Ferrer in the Forada Chapel. Veneration of Saint Roc increased greatly here when the area was struck by the plague in 1652, and there is an 18th-century altarpiece dedicated to the saint

Partial view of the beach at Port des Torrent.

and featuring a carving of him and a statute of Saint Francis of Assisi. The upper section of the altarpiece has Salomonicas, the lower Corinthian. The patio of the church is a haven of peace where the elderly folk of the village gather under the shade of the porches to gain respite from the noise and bustle of the adjoining streets. On either side of the great Bay of Sant Antoni, closed off by the **Island of Sa Cunillera** where, according to legend, the famous Carthaginian general Hannibal was born, are many beaches, such as those of **Cala Grassió** to the north and **Port d'es Torrent** and **Cala Bassa** to the south. Tiny Cala Salada is reached after Cap Negret and Punta Galera. Nearby, in a spot known as Ses Fontanelles, on the southern slopes of Cerro Nunó, is a rocky cave known as La Cova des Vi. Here, in 1917, the famous prehistorian H. Breuill discovered a number of enigmatic paintings difficult to interpret. These are the only cave paintings known on the islands. In 1994, the Department of Culture, Education and Heritage of the Ibiza and Formentera Island Council began to rehabilitate the site, which was becoming degraded. Although the cave is now closed for safety reasons, the visitor can still obtain a clear idea of what this singular historic monument contains thanks to an exhibition of panels reproducing the paintings, accompanied by explanatory texts. Another monument of historic importance is less than two kilometres to the north of Sant Antoni. This is the catacomb or underground chapel of Santa Agnès, discovered in 1907 and declared a monument of historic and artistic interest in 1964. It was restored and opened to the public in 1981. The church appears to date back to early Christian times and it has been ascertained that Christians continued to worship here during the time of the Moorish occupation. Inside were discovered many objects dating to the Punic, Roman and Moorish periods. According to legend, a wooden statue of Saint Ines was found in the church in the 16th

Aerial view of Cala Bassa.

Cala Comte.

century. This was taken several times to the Parish Church of Sant Antoni, but always returned to the cave. Just eight kilometres inland from Sant Antoni is the tiny village of **Sant Rafel,** where many artists have established their pottery workshops. Here, visitors can admire and purchase a variety of objects ranging from terra-cotta vases reproducing Punic models to avant-garde creations, not to mention the typical souvenir of a reproduction of a white Ibizan

Cala Codolar.

*Overall view of
Cala Tarida.*

Cala Molí.

Cala Vedella.

house. The village also features a splendid architecture jewel in the form of its parish church, standing on a small hill and commanding panoramic views of the surrounding countryside to the acropolis of Eivissa, standing out on the horizon. The church was built in the 18th century, commissioned by Bishop Abad y Lasierra. The choir was added and the rectory extended in the following century. Outstanding features include the flying buttresses of the nave, the singled-arched porch beside the main doorway and the turricular bullrush crowned by a small dome. Returning to Sant Antoni and leaving the great bay behind us to the south, we come to an endless succession of sandy beaches, notably **Cala Comte, Cala Codolar, Cala Tarida, Cala Molí, Cala Vedella** and **Cala Carbó.** We can break our journey with visits to the tower known as the Torre de Comte or Torre d'en Rovira, which stands on the point of the same name. Its strategic site commands lovely views of the tiny islands of S'Espartar, Ses Bledes, S'Illa des Bosc and Sa Cunillera, this last

Aerial view of Cala Carbó.

with a small quay and a lighthouse at the northernmost point. The Torre de Comte was built in the second half of the 18th century by García Martínez according to plans drawn up by the engineer Ballester. This is a tower of the first class, that is, the largest of others of its type. The original door is still conserved on the first floor, as well as the four brackets of the machicolation. Despite the poor road, the trip to **Cala d'Hort** should, under no circumstance, be missed. The waters of this beach of thick sand are especially clear and clean, and the terraces of its restaurants offer the most spectacular views in Ibiza: the «fantastic rocky tooth», as writer Josep Pla described the pinnacle on **Isla Vedrà,** rising from the dark waters to a height of 381 metres, flanked by the tiny **Islet of Vedranell.** Nearby is the Punic-Roman settlement of Ses Països de Cala d'Hort, founded in the second half of the 5th century BC and which continued to exist during the times of Roman and Byzantine domination, right up to the beginning of the 8th century. The site was exca-

The Isle of Vedrà.

vated in 1917 and 1982-1985. It consists of a large building used as a dwelling and for the development of different agricultural activities, and of two necropolises, one Punic and the other Byzantine. In the 1st century AD, the main building acquired the structure and proportions of a true Roman villa, reaching a size of approximately 900 square metres, the whole arranged around around a large central courtyard. Our route now takes us to **Sant Josep,** the road winding around the sierra of the same name and whose highest peak, the **Pico de Sa Talaia** is, at 475 metres, also the highest point on the island. The town of Sant Josep features a fine 18th-century parish church, restored after the Spanish Civil War. The front is plain and simple, its only external adornment the three crosses of Calvary on one side of the porch and a sundial at the top of the building. Inside - a nave covered by a barrel vault - the church is splendidly decorated with tiles, frescoes, a magnificent high altar

Sant Josep: view of the town, and the altarpiece dedicated to Saint Joseph.

and paintings on the wooden pulpit representing the Mysteries, by José Sánchez Ocaña in 1763. A few years after the completion of this church, in 1731, the Altarpiece of Sant Josep, by the Majorcan maestro Pere Bosch, was installed. This was destroyed by fire in 1936, and only the baroque statue of the saint survived. With over 10,000 inhabitants, Sant Josep is the fourth most highly populated district on the island, as well as the largest in size. Festivals of folklore take place in its central square every summer,

Beach at Ses Salines.

giving visitors the chance to admire local costumes and the typical dances of the island. Also interesting is the Sarganta art gallery, just a few metres from the church, featuring the naòf paintings of the Brazilian artist Yussara de Oliveira, reproducing Ibizan motifs and the books of stories by Gastao Heberle. Just over three kilometres from Sant Josep is the pretty village of **Sant Agustí des Vedrà,** one of the most characteristic in the interior of the island, its church perched on a hill sur-

rounded by 17th and 18th century rural dwellings, now occupied by cafés, restaurants and an art gallery. The path southwards beginning opposite the Church of Sant Josep leads to the solitary Hermitage of **Es Cubells** (19th century), standing on a promontory, and the recondite **Cala Llentrisca,** until recently only accessible by sea. Some five kilometres in the direction of Eivissa is **Cova Santa,** a cave whose underground chambers contain a fantastic world made up of stalagmites and sta-

Church of Sant Jordi.

lactites. The cave has a depth of around 25 metres and was discovered in the 15th century, when it was used by the local country people as a refuge during pirate attacks. Continuing southwards from this cave, we come to **Sa Caleta,** a peninsula between **Playa des Codolar** and the **Puig des Jondal** This is the site of the remains of the first settlement founded by the Phoenicians in the 7th century BC. Visitors can contemplate the so-called «south quarter» of this township, featuring eight dwelling units, narrow streets and irregular-shaped little squares. Before returning to Eivissa, we cannot but take the detour to **Ses Salines,** first passing the beautiful Church of **Sant Jordi** with its defensive elements, its battlemented flat roof giving the building the air of a church-castle. Its origins go back to the 13th century, though the chapel built in those times by the salt-miners who inhabited this part of the island was replaced by a different building in subsequent years. The side chapels, crowned

View of Platja d'en Bossa.

by graceful domes date to the 18th century. The interior of the church was extensively reformed during the 19th century. South of the airport, passing through the small town of **Sant Francesc,** we enter the salt-mining region. The salt mines are one of the first images of the island to be impressed on the memory of the traveller arriving by air in Ibiza, along with the windmills which in years gone by transformed grain into flour and pumped water to the surface. The salt mines were exploited since ancient times, by Phoenicians, Romans and Moors, constituting one of the island's main resources for many centuries, allowing both the population and the *Universitat* (system of self-government) to pay for imports of grain and defence materials. After passing into the hands of the Spanish crown during the reign of Philip V, the salt mines were sold to a private company. They now occupy and area of 400 hectares with 40 dykes and produce over 100,000 tonnes of salt per year for export to different

Overall view of Platja d'en Bossa.

northern European countries. In recent decades, the mines have been the subject of numerous revindications on the part of ecologists to prevent these lands being developed. The beauty of this landscape, which reaches its maximum point at sunset, will captivate any visitor. And it is in cosmopolitan **Platja de Ses Salines,** where a veritable legion of beautiful bathers recline in the sun after their exhausting nocturnal escapades. More peaceful is **Platja d'Es Cavallet,** facing eastwards, often used by nudists. At La Punta de Ses Portes, a point separating the two beaches which is also the southernmost point on the island, stands the Torre de Ses Portes, a tower whose existence is recorded since at least 1620, though it may have been built as long ago as the 16th century. To return to Eivissa, we can take the same road or, leaving the Puig des Corb Marí and Torre de sa Sal Rossa mountains on our right, drive around the huge tourist resorts of **Platja d'En Boss** and **Figueretes.**

Platja d'en Bossa.

Sport and Leisure

Ibizan nights are famous, offering as they do a wide range of diversions: its casino, its shows, its concerts, its many discotheques and parties are well known. The starting-point in the so-called «night-time circuit» are the bars and cafés of La Marina, where by sunset the first night-birds have gathered to wait for the arrival of the animators at the great discotheques such as Ku, Pacha or Amnesia, handing out invitations. These centres of nocturnal entertainment, many of them several kilometres outside the city, are veritable festivals of beauty and youth and the scene of the most exciting parties and shows. For those seeking more peaceful diversion, Ibiza celebrates its International Festival of Classical Music every August. Another important event is the «Ibizan Fashion Show», organised in the first week of July. World-renowned, Ad-Lib

Figueretes.

fashion, created in Ibiza during the 1970s under the slogan «wear what you want, but with taste», still attracts fashion designers from all parts.

Ibiza and Formentera, thanks to their geographical situation, their clean waters and their splendid climate, are a paradise for lovers of water sports of all kinds. Windsurfing, sailing, water skiing and underwater exploration are just some of the sports available here. Swimmers seeking clean, white sand and crystal-clear water will find broad beaches and hidden coves, whilst sailing enthusiasts can choose among ten pleasure ports and countless magnificent anchorages in the tiny islets and sheltered bays of Las Pitiusas. Tennis and horse-riding facilities are also available in different parts of the islands, whilst golfers can choose between two courses (the Ibiza I Golf Club, with nine holes, and the 18-hole Ibiza II Golf Club) in the Roca Llisa residential zone.

Folklore

Ibiza and Formentera still conserve their own folklore, including traditional music and dances, and older countrywomen can still be seen dressed in traditional black dress, the working clothes which are replaced on special occasions by the festive costume, adorned with splendid «emprendadas». The men's costume is much more austere, absolutely without ostentation, excepting the silk handkerchief they wear around the neck, the wide waistband and the dark red «barret», or cap. Men and women alike wear the typical pita «espardenyes», sandals. Thus attired, the dancing couples move to the music of the wooden flute, «castanyoles», castanets, and the «xeremía», or flageolet, in a dance full of age-old symbolism and whose meaning is explained to the spectators in the patio of the Church of Sant Miquel de Balansat every Thursday. The most popular dances are the «sa llarga», the «sa curta» and the «ball de ses dotze rodades», in which the slow, circling movement of the women, who barely lift their feet from the ground, contrast with the huge leaps made by the men. During the festivities in honour of Saint James, the patron saint of Formentera, the traditional «Ball pagès», or country ball, takes place, along with the «tirada dels galls» and «sa cantada».

Gastronomy

The most popular dishes in the local cuisine are the «sofrit pagès», made with different types of meat, sausages and spices, the «arròs de matançes», a rice dish, and the «coles a la ibicenca». Fish dishes include the «bullit de peix», the «burrida de ratjada» and «rao», found almost exclusively in the waters of Formentera. Recommended desserts include the fresh cheese made in the traditional way and served with honey and nuts, «oreietes anisadas», «flaó» (a cake made with cheese, honey and almonds) and «graixonera», tart made from the most famous local pastry, the «ensaimada». These islands are also famed for their herbal liquors, particularly the typical Frígola (made from thyme), taken by Ibizans as a digestive or at any time of the day.

Graixonera and Frígola.

Oreietes.

Sofrit pagès.

Aerial view of Formentera.

Formentera

A boat journey of scarcely an hour takes us from bustling Ibiza to peaceful **Formentera** which with an area of 82 km², has a population of just over 5,000. On this tiny island, the bicycle is the ideal form of transport. The point of arrival is the port of **La Savina,** mooring-place of luxury yachts and elegant sailing ships as well as passenger ferries and fishing boats. The main road to **La Mola** starts out from this tiny town, containing restaurants, hotels and bicycle hire

shops. La Mola is a flat meseta lying 192 metres above sea level some 19 kilometres to the eastern end of the island. Formentera is made up of Miocene platforms whose collapse, together with the erosion caused by the sea, created a coastline which becomes lower at the ends with long sandy beaches in the middle. Prehistoric remains on the island, thought to have been first populated some 4,000 years ago, include the megalithic burial ground of Ca Na Costa, close to El Pujols. The island's name comes from that

*Formentera:
views of its
beaches.*

*Formentera:
La Sabina
port.*

Es Pujols beach.

given to it by the Romans, Frumentum, due to its abundance of wheat fields. There are remains of Roman buildings in Ca'n Blai, close to Es Caló. After being conquered successively by Vandals, Byzantines and Moors, Formentera was colonised by Catalans, who dwelt here until the beginning of the 15th century, at which point the island was left uninhabited until the 18th century. The defensive towers built at strategic points of the coast to look out for pirate attacks, frequent here, form part of the landscape, and the island's

old windmills, formerly used to grind grain or salt, are also highly picturesque. Close to La Savina are **Los Estanys de Ses Salines,** a patchwork of walls and salt pools which, according to the time of the year and light conditions, present incredible tones of pink, mauve and purple. Northwards from this point stretches out an area of land covered in sand dunes, pine trees and savins from where the islets of **Espalmador** and **Espardell** can be seen, close to this **Punta des Trocadors.** On either side of this headland are

Church of Sant Francesc Xavier.

magnificent beaches of fine sand whilst the interior contains the **Estany Pudent,** a lake designated a «Natural Area of Particular Interest» due to its vegetation and birdlife. The road around this lake and past the **Llevant beach** takes us to **Els Pujols,** the most important tourist resort on the island. Here we can pause in our journey to visit the megalithic monument of Ca Na Costa, excavated between 1975 and 1977. The site produced many important findings, such as the «archer's bracelet» and human remains dating back to around 1600 BC according to C-14 radiocarbon testing. The main road leads now to **Sant Francesc Xavier,** administrative centre and meeting-point for locals and visitors alike. Every morning, craftsmen and women install a market in the square containing the 18th-century fortified church and in the surrounding streets. Not far off is the tiny Chapel of Sa Tanca Vella, whose origins go back to the 14th century, when the inhabitants of the flat part of the island must have felt sufficiently important to petition the archbishop of Tarra-

La Sabina port.

Illetes beach.

Cala Saona.

gona for permission to build a chapel close to the area known as the Cova de Sant Valero. After the repopulation of the island in the early-18th century, the chapel was no longer large enough to hold all the worshippers and in 1726 building began of a new church devoted to Saint Francis Xavier. Near to Sant Francesc is the point known as the **Cap de Barbaria,** where there are a lighthouse and a defensive tower standing on the cliffs of a 113-metre high meseta. Here, a path leads to **Cala Saona,** a pretty beach on the rocky western coast whose waters and sands provide a resting-ground for local fishing boats. The centre of the island, around **Sant Ferran,** is characterised by a landscape of ploughed fields between stone walls, fig trees and typical little houses covered in vines. In order to taste the wine of Formentera, it is necessary to visit one of these farmhouses where the wine produced cannot be found in the local shops. In this landscape, women sit under the porches of their houses knitting typical pullovers made of local wool. Paths lead

Es Caló.

from the narrowest point of the island to the beaches of Mitjorn and
Es Arenals on the southern coast.
Before beginning the climb up to
the high plateau of La Mola, the
visitor should rest a while in the
little village of **Es Caló.** Nearby are
the remains of the Roman fortress
of Can Blai, excavated in the late-
1970s and consisting of a quad-
rangular site measuring 40 metres
along each side with five rectangular towers. Its structure indicates

Mitjorn beach.

that this is a classical fortification built on the edges of the Roman Empire in around the 5th century AD. The curving road up to La Mola runs through a forest zone to points commanding magnificent panoramic views of the entire island, Ibiza and the islet of Es Vedrà. The meseta of La Mola contains **Sa Talaia,** the highest point on Formentera, and the village of **Nostra Senyora del Pilar,** the home of many artists. South of the road leading to the eastern point of the high plateau we can see El Molí Vell de la Mola, a typical flour mill which, though it dates back to 1778, is still in a good state of repair and was recently acquired by the «Islas Baleares» Foundation. On the cliffs stands the La Mola lighthouse, where Jules Verne found the inspiration for one of his works and in whose memory stands a monolith, here, at the «end of the world».

La Mola lighthouse.

CONTENTS

IBIZA AND FORMENTERA:

1st Edition

I.S.B.N. 84-378-1754-4

Dep. Legal B. 15158-1996

Protegemos el bosque; papel procedente de cultivos forestales controlados
Wir schützen den Wald. Papier aus kontrollierten Forsten.
We protect our forests. The paper used comes from controlled forestry plantations
Nous sauvegardons la forêt: papier provenant de cultures forestières controlées

The printing of this book was comp
in the workshops of
FISA - ESCUDO DE ORO, S.A.
Palaudarias, 26 - Barcelona (Spa